A New way to Learn

અ બ ક

ABCs of Gujarati

Workbook

Chintan Gandhi

A Different Way

Learning to read and write a new language is an amazing endeavor that will benefit you beyond the new skill. Gujarati is a phonetic language with a script that is quite distinct from English. The **technique** of this workbook is **mirroring** the English alphabet, that you know so well. This technique will drastically simplify **Learning** the Gujarati Alphabet. With an easy pronunciation **exercise and practice**, you will amaze yourself with your progress!

Mirroring Technique

The Gujarati alphabet has been arranged into the A-Z order. I bet you can sing "A B C D E F G.... now I know my ABCs..." without thinking of it. Learning Gujarati in the same order will help you to associate the letters of this new language.

The example words used are English words and names. Sounding out words like America and Bus, will make the Gujarati alphabet sounds easier to remember.

Study Aids

Study aids work because they reinforce what you have learned in different manners. Get the companion app to this workbook: ***ABCs of Gujarati*** for iOS and Android. The app allows you to practice writing the letters, but also includes flashcards and matching game to test and reinforce your learning.

This workbook will help you to learn the Gujarati alphabet. I value your thoughts and comments, contact me at cdsngconsulting@gmail.com.

Chintan Gandhi

ISBN 978-1-7352782-1-6

Table of Contents

ABCs of Gujarati

In the following pages you will see the Gujarati alphabet, one letter at a time. Each Gujarati alphabet will be associated with its representative English letter and an English Word. The A-Z English letter will help your brain to associate the new Gujarati letter's script. The English word will allow you to identify the proper pronunciation. Then, each page will provide an ability to trace the letter several times and finally, practice writing the letter.

A few pieces of advice….

Make this fun!
Pronounce the letters out loud. Exaggerate the sounds!
Move your mouth. Take a video selfie as you practice.
Trace and practice writing the letters, repetition works.
Remember, there are no grades, or tests. You are doing this for **you**.
The Gujarati alphabet is not case sensitive, meaning there is only one set of letters to learn.

Practice a few letters at a time and repeat. The workbook is organized by lessons to guide you. Do not try to learn the entire alphabet in one day - it does not work. Take this slowly but consistently, and you will be set for the rest of your life.

You can do it!

Lesson 1 - ABC

અ	A	America
અ, A sounds like the "uh" in America.	**Learn It:**	

Learn It:

- Think of "A" in America.
- Imagine the sound.
- Pronounce it.
- Trace the letter, then write it.

અ અ અ અ અ અ અ

અ અ અ અ અ અ અ

અ

અ

Lesson 1 - ABC

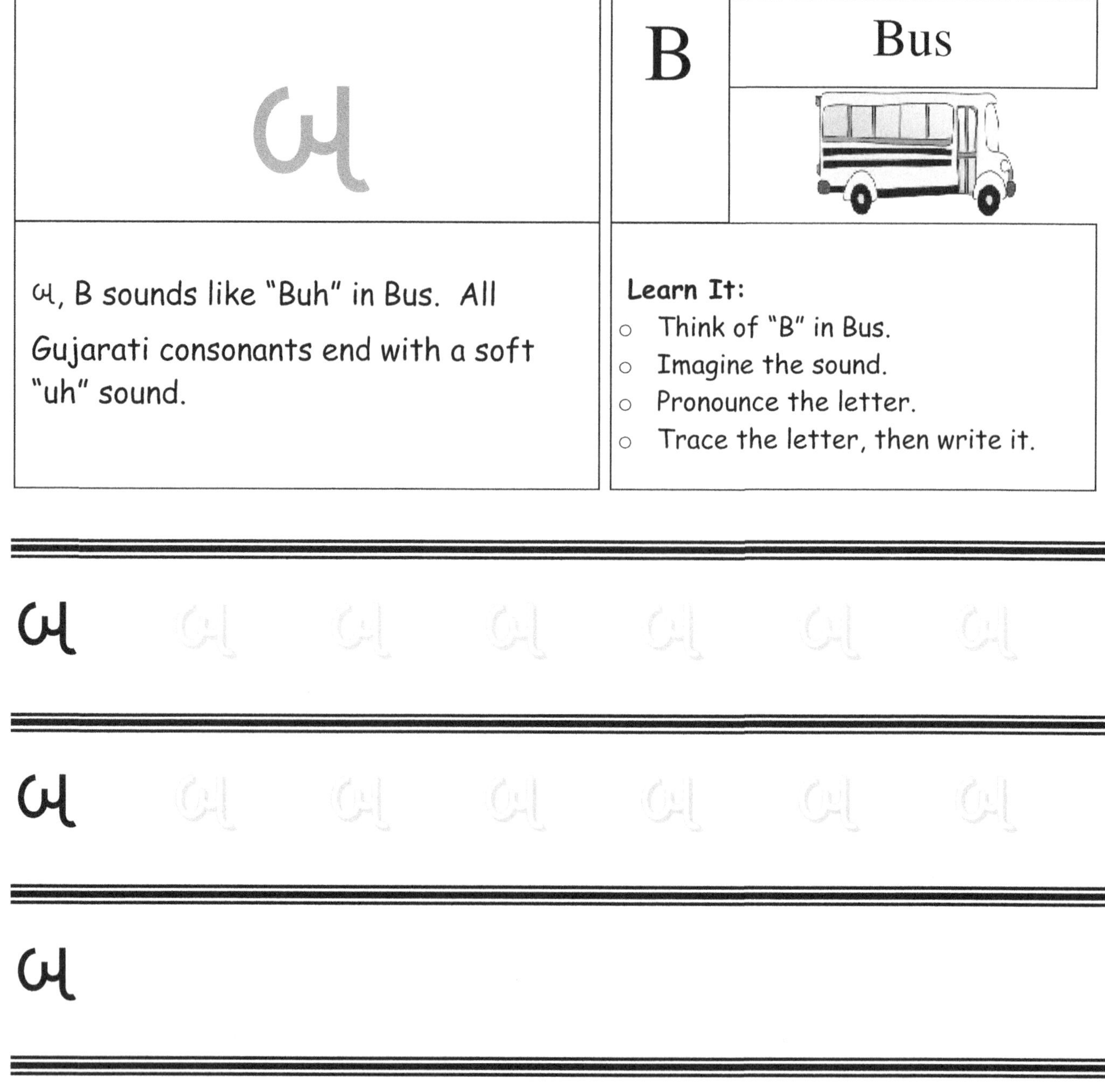

બ

B

Bus

બ, B sounds like "Buh" in Bus. All Gujarati consonants end with a soft "uh" sound.

Learn It:

- Think of "B" in Bus.
- Imagine the sound.
- Pronounce the letter.
- Trace the letter, then write it.

બ

બ

બ

બ

Lesson 1 - ABC

ભ	B 2	Bharat 

ભ, B2 sounds like "Bhuh" as in Bharat.

In Gujarati, many consonants have a secondary form, which are pronounced with an "huh" sound.

Learn It:

- Think of "Bh" in Bharat.
- Imagine the sound.
- Pronounce the letter.
- Trace the letter, then write it.

ભ ભ ભ ભ ભ ભ ભ

ભ ભ ભ ભ ભ ભ ભ

ભ

ભ

Lesson 1 - ABC

ચ	C	Chin

ચ, C in Gujarati sounds like "Ch" in Chin. In English, the letter C can sound like an S or a K. When an H is added, you get the "CH" sound.

Learn It:

- Think of "Ch" in Chin.
- Imagine the sound.
- Pronounce the letter,
- Trace the letter, then write it.

ચ ચ ચ ચ ચ ચ ચ

ચ ચ ચ ચ ચ ચ ચ

ચ

ચ

Lesson 1 - ABC

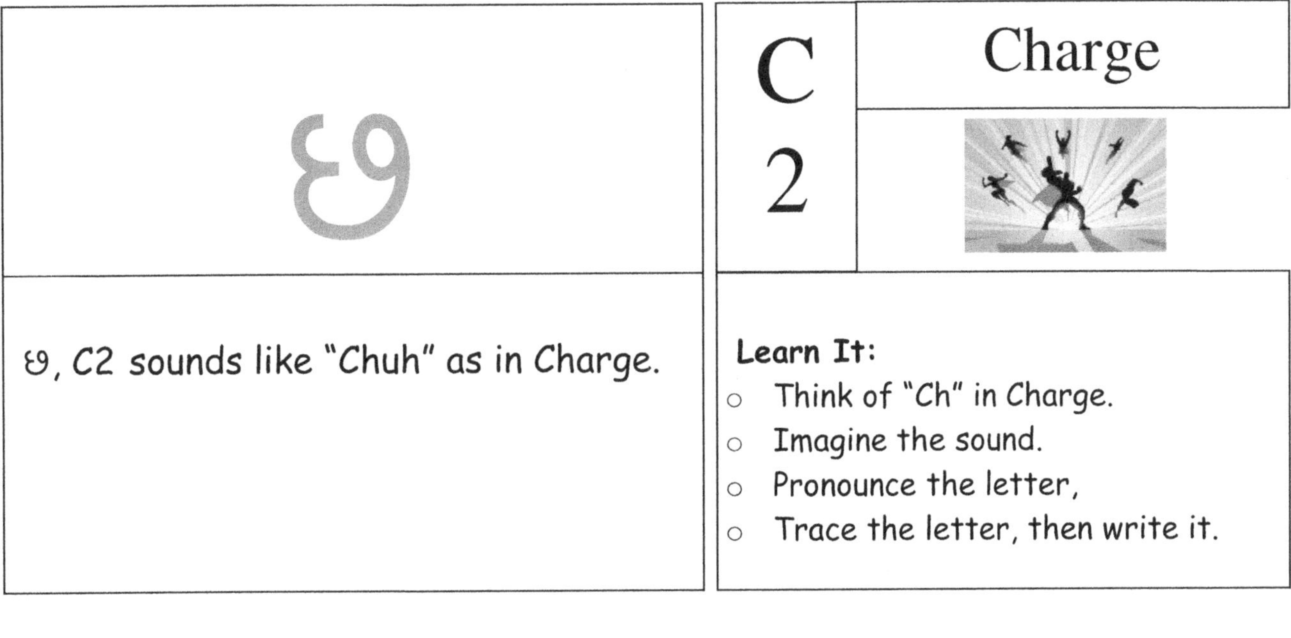

C
2

Charge

, C2 sounds like "Chuh" as in Charge.

Learn It:

- Think of "Ch" in Charge.
- Imagine the sound.
- Pronounce the letter,
- Trace the letter, then write it.

End of lesson.

Lesson 2 - D

દ	D	Duck
દ,D sounds like the "D" in Duck.	**Learn It:** ○ Think of "D" in Duck. ○ Imagine the sound. ○ Pronounce the letter, ○ Trace the letter, then write it.	

દ દ દ દ દ દ દ

દ દ દ દ દ દ દ

દ

દ

Lesson 2 - D

S	D 2	Dad 
S, D2 sound like "D" in "Dad". It sounds different than the "D" in Duck. Say Duck. Say Dad. Notice the difference.	**Learn It:** ○ Think of "D" in Dad. ○ Imagine the sound. ○ Pronounce the letter, ○ Trace the letter, then write it.	

S S S S S S S

S S S S S S S

S

S

Lesson 2 - D

ધ	D 3	Dharma *Dharma*

ધ, D3 is this "huh" version of the letter D. The main example for ધ "Dh" is the word **Dharma**, pronounce it with the "h" sound and not as Darma.

Learn It:

- Think of "Dh" in Dharma.
- Imagine the sound.
- Pronounce the letter,
- Trace the letter, then write it.

ધ ધ ધ ધ ધ ધ ધ

ધ ધ ધ ધ ધ ધ ધ

ધ

ધ

Lesson 2 - D

ધ	D 4	the *the*
ધ, D4 sounds like the word "the", or "the" in father.	**Learn It:** ○ Think of "the". ○ Imagine the sound. ○ Pronounce the letter, ○ Trace the letter, then write it.	

ધ ધ ધ ધ ધ ધ ધ

ધ ધ ધ ધ ધ ધ ધ

ધ

ધ

End of lesson.

Lesson 3 - EFG

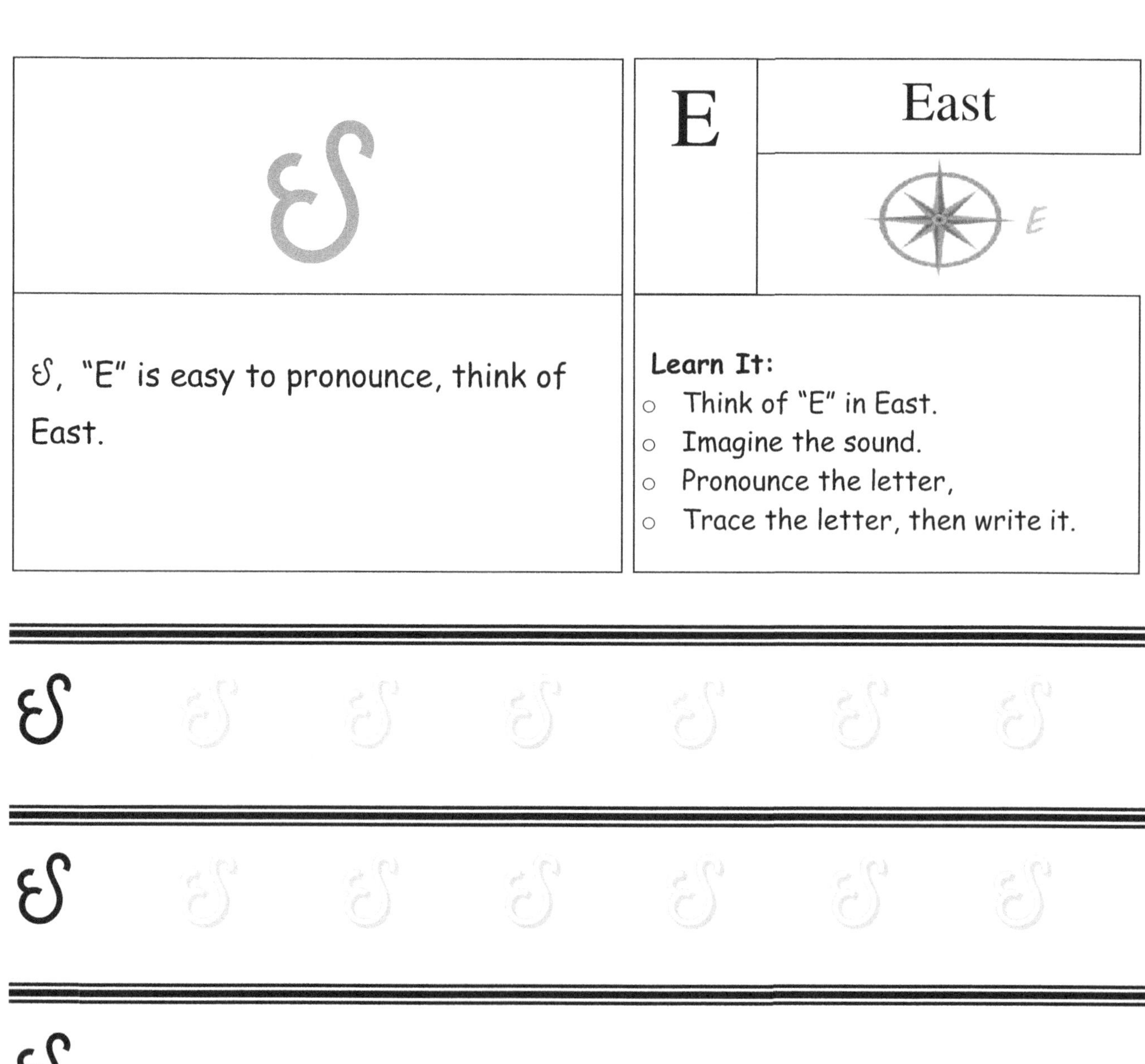

ઈ

ઈ

Lesson 3 - EFG

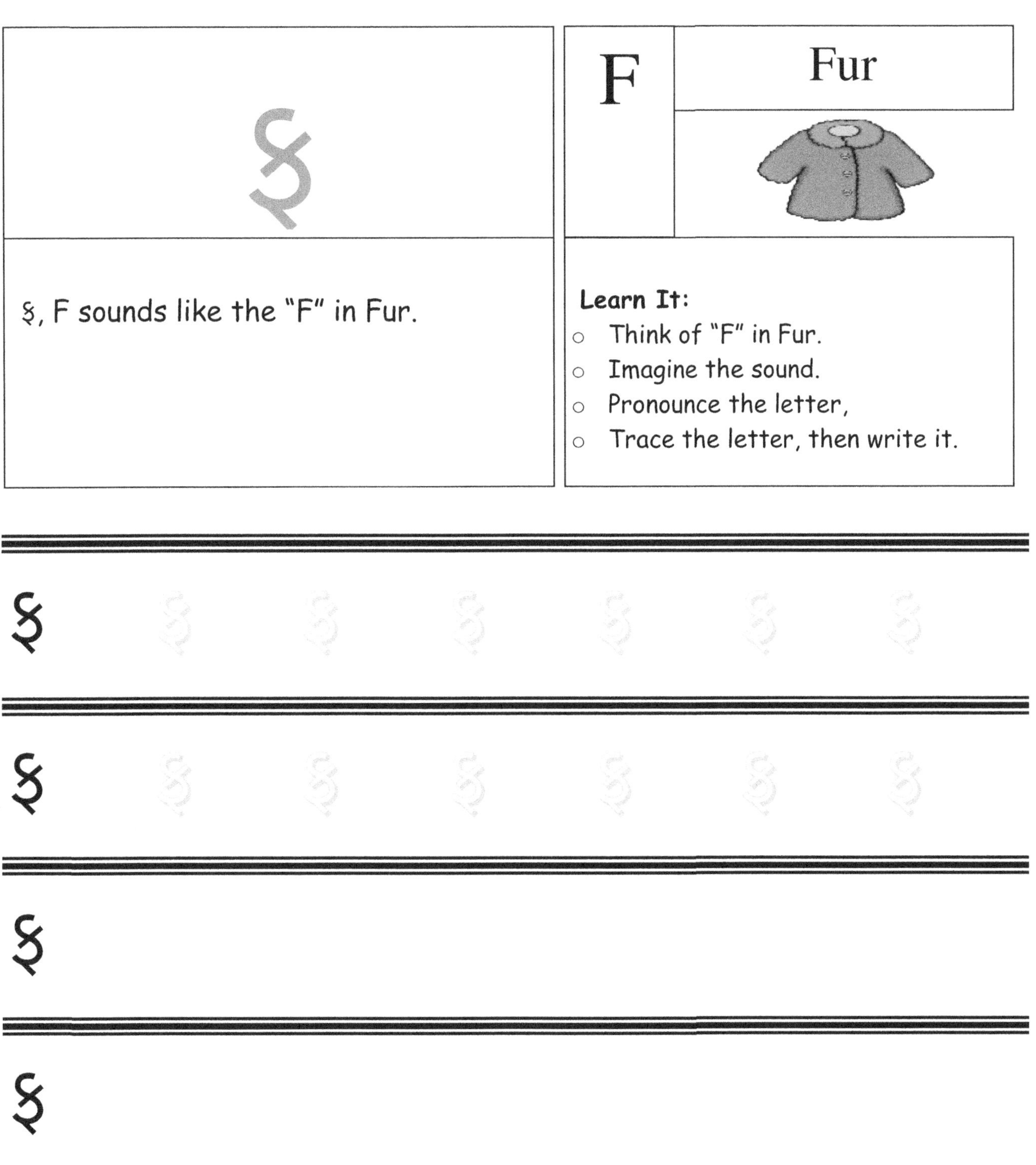
ડ
F
Fur
ડ, F sounds like the "F" in Fur.
Learn It:
Think of "F" in Fur.
Imagine the sound.
Pronounce the letter,
Trace the letter, then write it.
ડ
ડ
ડ
ડ

Lesson 3 - EFG

ગ	G	Gum

ગ, G is the "G" sound in Gum.

Learn It:

- Think of "G" in Gum.
- Imagine the sound.
- Pronounce the letter,
- Trace the letter, then write it.

ગ ગ ગ ગ ગ ગ ગ

ગ ગ ગ ગ ગ ગ ગ

ગ

ગ

Lesson 3 - EFG

ઘ	G 2	Ghost
ઘ, G2 is the "huh" version of G to make "Ghuh" sound as in Ghost.	**Learn It:** ○ Think of "Gh" in Ghost. ○ Imagine the sound. ○ Pronounce the letter, ○ Trace the letter, then write it.	

ઘ ઘ ઘ ઘ ઘ ઘ ઘ

ઘ ઘ ઘ ઘ ઘ ઘ ઘ

ઘ

ઘ

End of lesson.

Lesson 4 - HIJ

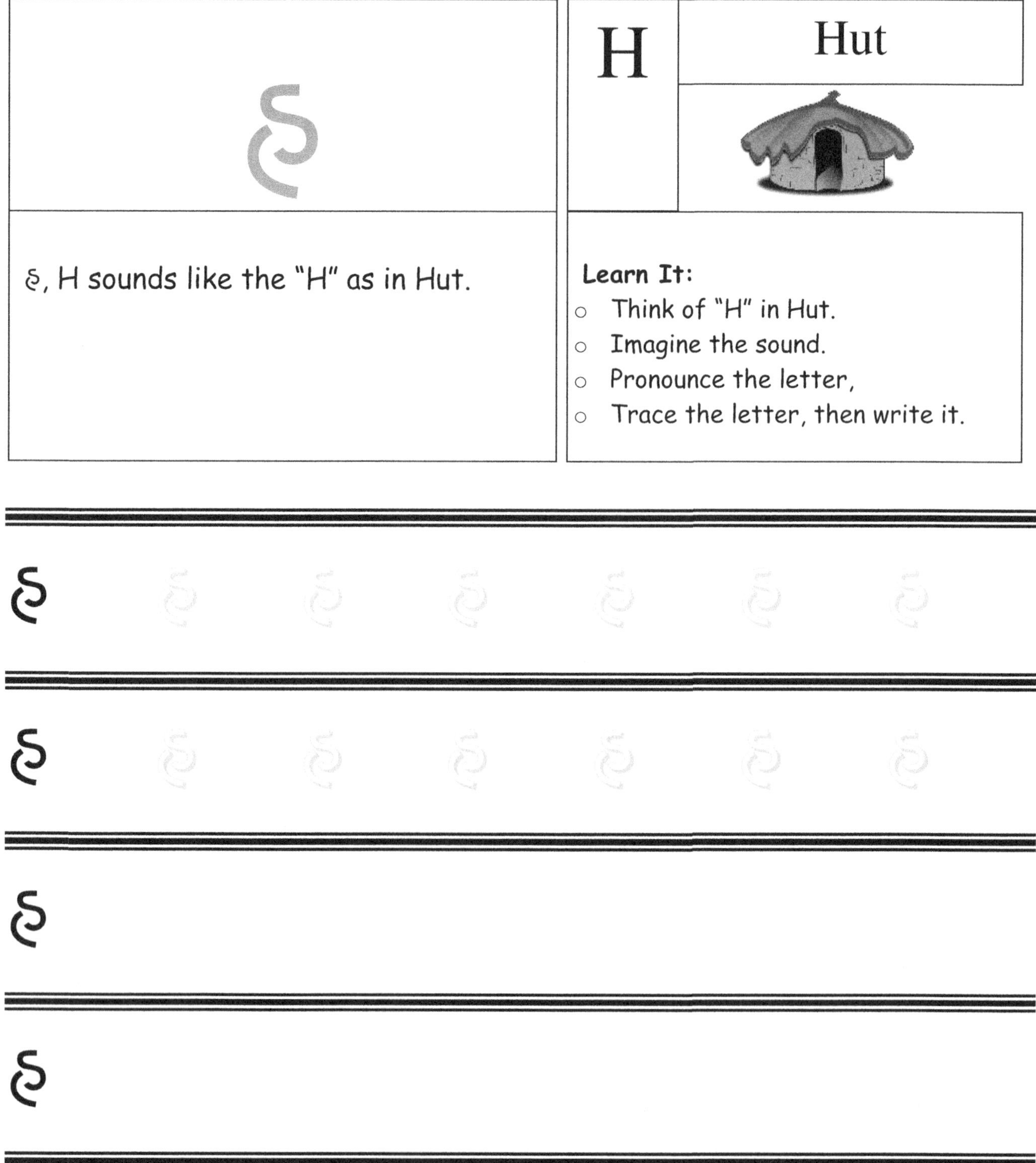
હ
H
Hut
હ, H sounds like the "H" as in Hut.
Learn It:
Think of "H" in Hut.
Imagine the sound.
Pronounce the letter,
Trace the letter, then write it.
હ
હ
હ
હ

Lesson 4 - HIJ

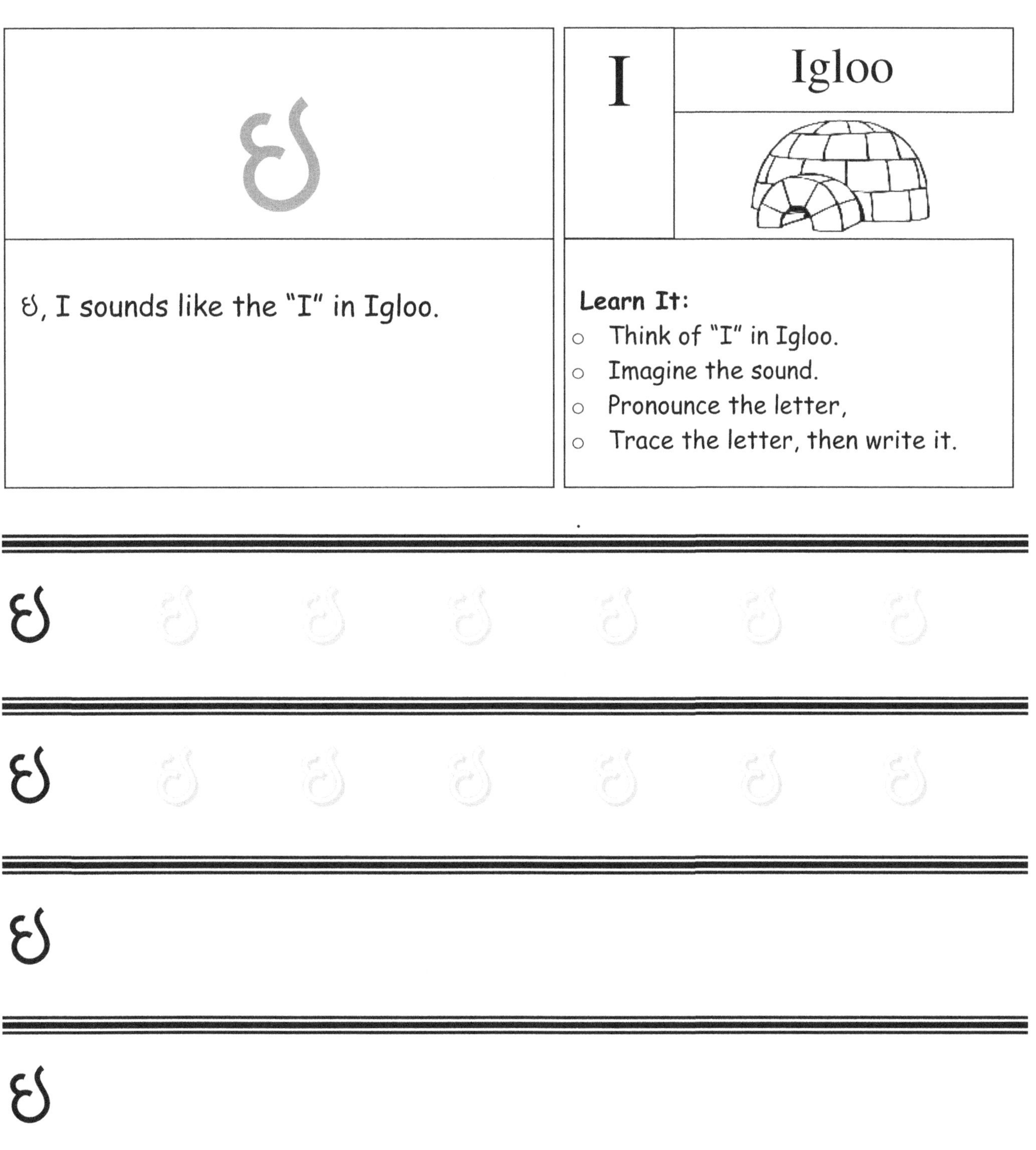
ઇ
I
Igloo
ઇ, I sounds like the "I" in Igloo.
Learn It:
Think of "I" in Igloo.
Imagine the sound.
Pronounce the letter,
Trace the letter, then write it.
ઇ
ઇ
ઇ
ઇ

Lesson 4 - HIJ

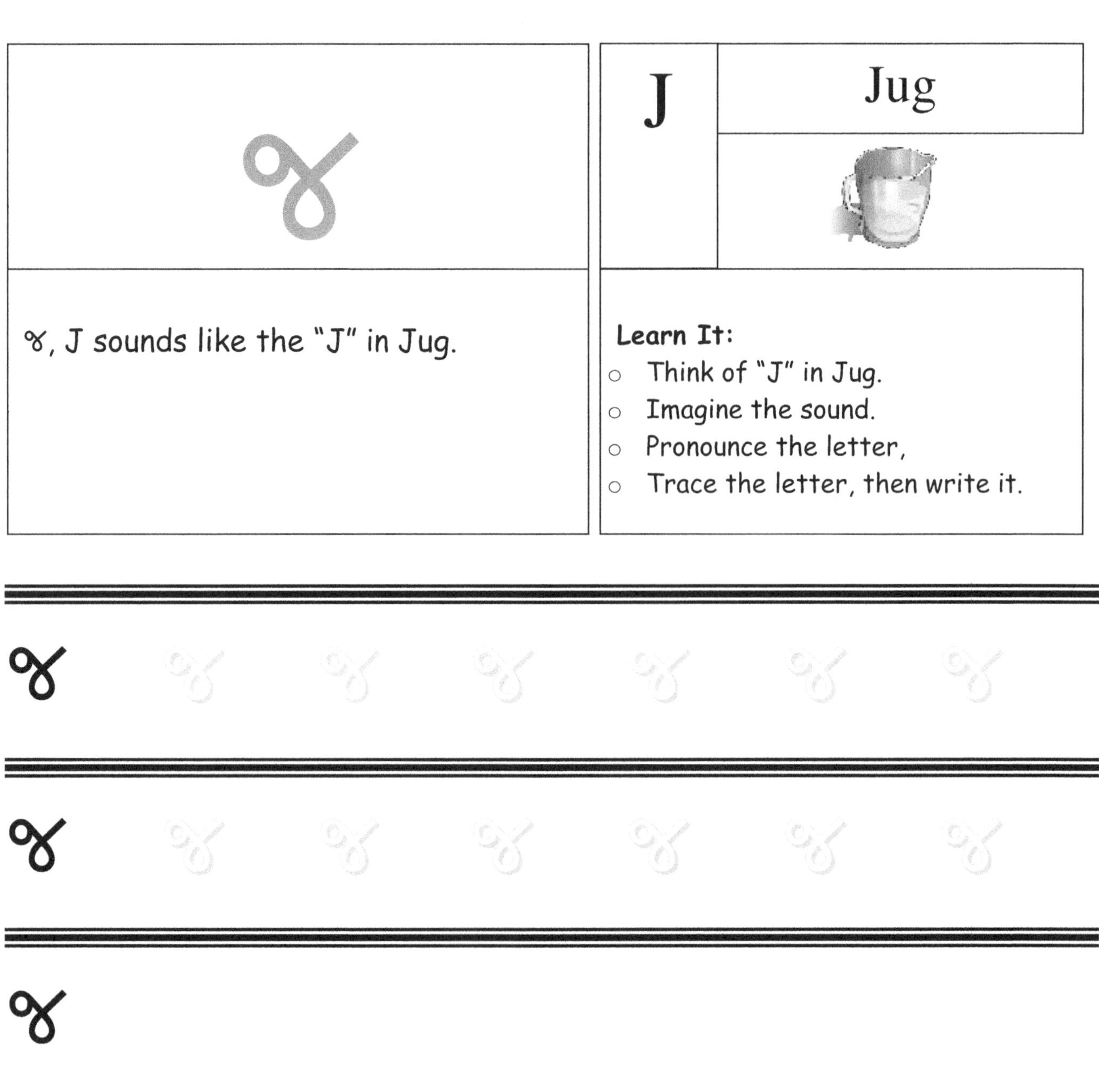

જ	J	Jug

જ, J sounds like the "J" in Jug.

Learn It:

- Think of "J" in Jug.
- Imagine the sound.
- Pronounce the letter,
- Trace the letter, then write it.

જ

જ

જ

જ

End of lesson.

Lesson 5 - KL

ક	K	Kazoo

ક, K sounds like the "K" in Kazoo. The letter C and Q words such as Cut, Cave, and Queen can also be written with the Gujarati ક, K.

Learn It:

- Think of "K" in Kazoo.
- Imagine the sound.
- Pronounce the letter,
- Trace the letter, then write it.

ક ક ક ક ક ક ક

ક ક ક ક ક ક ક

ક

ક

Lesson 5 - KL

ખ	K 2	Khan 
ખ, K2 is the "Kh" sound as in Khan, and Cousin.	**Learn It:** ○ Think of "Kh" in Khan. ○ Imagine the sound. ○ Pronounce the letter, ○ Trace the letter, then write it.	

ખ ખ ખ ખ ખ ખ ખ

ખ ખ ખ ખ ખ ખ ખ

ખ

ખ

Lesson 5 - KL

ક્ષ	K 3	Kshatriya

ક્ષ, K3 sounds like "Ksh" as in Kshatriya. The letter X words such as X-ray can also be written with the Gujarati ક્ષ, Ksh.

Learn It:

- Think of "Ksh" in Kshatriya.
- Imagine the sound.
- Pronounce the letter,
- Trace the letter, then write it.

ક્ષ ક્ષ ક્ષ ક્ષ ક્ષ ક્ષ ક્ષ

ક્ષ ક્ષ ક્ષ ક્ષ ક્ષ ક્ષ ક્ષ

ક્ષ

ક્ષ

Lesson 5 - KL

લ	L	London
લ, L sounds like the "L" in London.	**Learn It:** ○ Think of "L" in London. ○ Imagine the sound. ○ Pronounce the letter, ○ Trace the letter, then write it.	

લ લ લ લ લ લ લ

લ લ લ લ લ લ લ

લ

લ

Lesson 5 - KL

ળ	L 2	a(l)a
		a(l)a

ળ, L2 sounds like "a(l)a", with your tongue going to the back and curving. Ask a native speaker or use the ABCs of Gujarati app to hear the sound.

Learn It:
- Think of "a(l)a".
- Imagine the sound.
- Pronounce the letter,
- Trace the letter, then write it.

ળ ળ ળ ળ ળ ળ ળ

ળ ળ ળ ળ ળ ળ ળ

ળ

ળ

End of lesson.

Lesson 6 - MNOP

મ	M	Mother

મ, M sounds like the "M" in Mother.

Learn It:

- Think of "M" in Mother.
- Imagine the sound.
- Pronounce the letter,
- Trace the letter, then write it.

મ મ મ મ મ મ મ

મ મ મ મ મ મ મ

મ

મ

Lesson 6 - MNOP

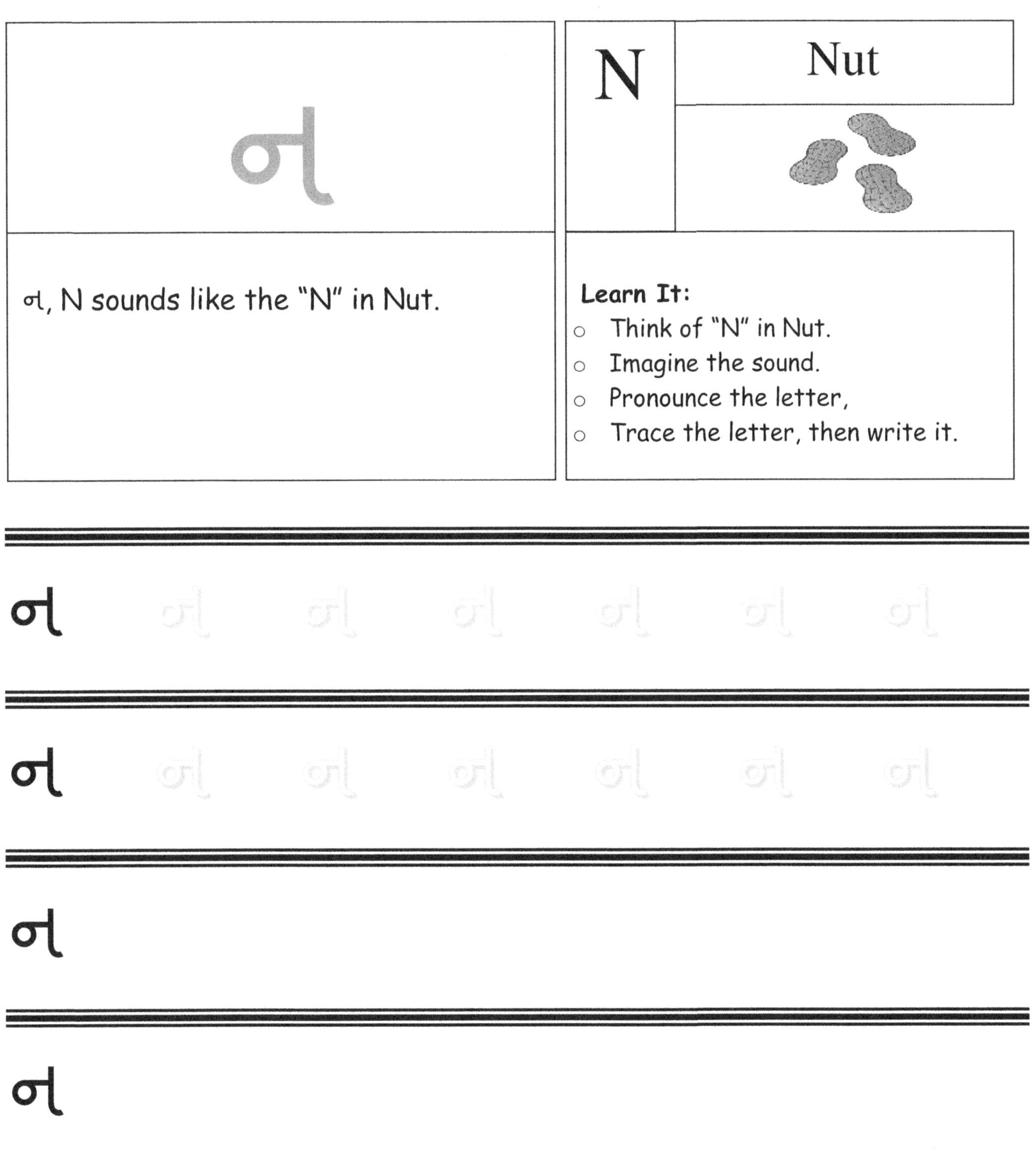

ન, N sounds like the "N" in Nut.

Learn It:

- Think of "N" in Nut.
- Imagine the sound.
- Pronounce the letter,
- Trace the letter, then write it.

ન

ન

ન

ન

Lesson 6 - MNOP

ણ	N 2	a(n)a *a(n)a*

ણ, N2 sounds like "a(n)a", with your tongue going to the back and curving. Ask a native speaker or use the ABCs of Gujarati app to hear the sound.

Learn It:

- Think of "a(n)a".
- Imagine the sound.
- Pronounce the letter,
- Trace the letter, then write it.

ણ ણ ણ ણ ણ ણ ણ

ણ ણ ણ ણ ણ ણ ણ

ણ

ણ

Lesson 6 - MNOP

O	Okra

ઓ, O sounds like the "O" in Okra. It is written like the A symbol, with an additional straight line and a backtick above the line.

Learn It:

- Think of "O" in Okra.
- Imagine the sound.
- Pronounce the letter,
- Trace the letter, then write it.

ઓ ઓ ઓ ઓ ઓ ઓ ઓ

ઓ ઓ ઓ ઓ ઓ ઓ ઓ

ઓ

ઓ

Lesson 6 - MNOP

પ	P	Puppy

પ, P sounds like the first "P" in Puppy.

Learn It:

- Think of "P" in Puppy.
- Imagine the sound.
- Pronounce the letter,
- Trace the letter, then write it.

પ પ પ પ પ પ પ

પ પ પ પ પ પ પ

પ

પ

End of lesson.

Lesson 7 - QRS

ર	R	Run

ર, R sounds like the "R" in Run.

Learn It:

- Think of "R" in Run.
- Imagine the sound.
- Pronounce the letter,
- Trace the letter, then write it.

ર ર ર ર ર ર ર

ર ર ર ર ર ર ર

ર

ર

Lesson 7 - QRS

સ	S	Sun

સ, S sounds like the "S" in Sun.

Learn It:
- Think of "S" in Sun.
- Imagine the sound.
- Pronounce the letter,
- Trace the letter, then write it.

સ સ સ સ સ સ સ

સ સ સ સ સ સ સ

સ

સ

Lesson 7 - QRS

શ	S 2	Ship 
શ, S2 sounds like the "Sh" in "Ship".	**Learn It:** ○ Think of "Sh" in Ship. ○ Imagine the sound. ○ Pronounce the letter, ○ Trace the letter, then write it.	

શ શ શ શ શ શ શ

શ શ શ શ શ શ શ

શ

શ

Lesson 7 - QRS

ષ

S
3

Shark

ષ, S3 sounds like the "Sha" in Shark.

Learn It:

- Think of "Sha" in Shark.
- Imagine the sound.
- Pronounce the letter,
- Trace the letter, then write it.

ષ ષ ષ ષ ષ ષ ષ

ષ ષ ષ ષ ષ ષ ષ

ષ

ષ

End of lesson.

Lesson 8 - T

ત	T	Tim *Tim*
ત, T sounds like the "T" in Tim. This is a soft "t" sound.	**Learn It:** ○ Think of "T" in Tim. ○ Imagine the sound. ○ Pronounce the letter, ○ Trace the letter, then write it.	

ત ત ત ત ત ત ત

ત ત ત ત ત ત ત

ત

ત

Lesson 8 - T

ટ

S	Tom
2	*Tom*

ટ, T2 sounds like the "T" in Tom. This is a hard "T" sound.

Learn It:

- Think of "T" in Tom.
- Imagine the sound.
- Pronounce the letter,
- Trace the letter, then write it.

ટ ટ ટ ટ ટ ટ ટ

ટ ટ ટ ટ ટ ટ ટ

ટ

ટ

Lesson 8 - T

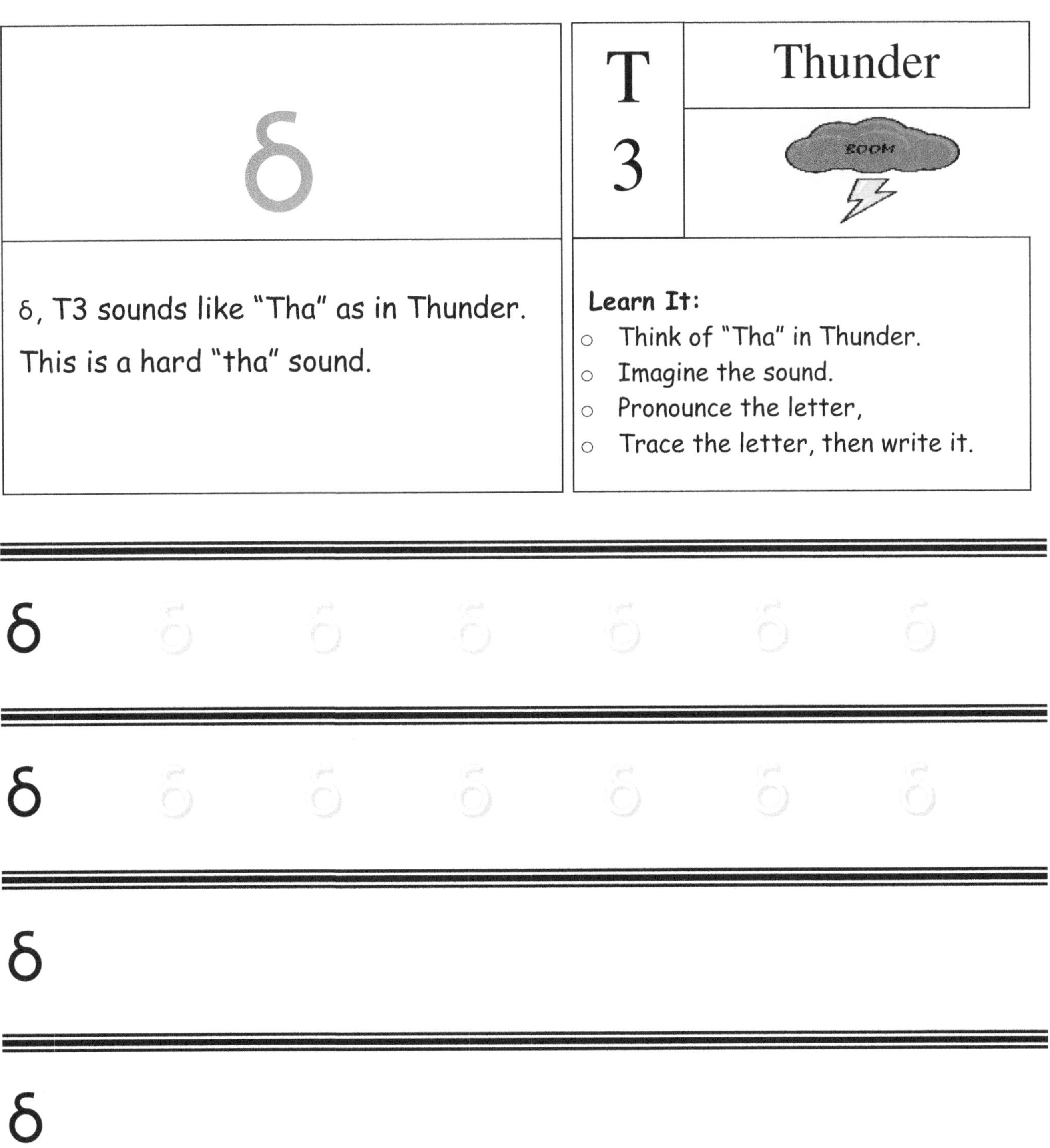
δ
T
3
Thunder
BOOM
δ, T3 sounds like "Tha" as in Thunder.
This is a hard "tha" sound.
Learn It:
Think of "Tha" in Thunder.
Imagine the sound.
Pronounce the letter,
Trace the letter, then write it.
δ
δ
δ
δ

Lesson 8 - T

થ	T 4	Think 

થ, T4 sounds like "Th" as in Think. This is a long and soft "th" sound.

Learn It:
- Think of "Th" in Think.
- Imagine the sound.
- Pronounce the letter,
- Trace the letter, then write it.

થ થ થ થ થ થ થ

થ થ થ થ થ થ થ

થ

થ

Lesson 8 - T

ત્ર

T

5

Tres

ત્ર, T5 sounds like "Tr" as in Tres. This is a conjunction of T and a rolling R sound.

Learn It:

- Think of "tr" in Tres.
- Imagine the sound.
- Pronounce the letter,
- Trace the letter, then write it.

ત્ર

ત્ર

ત્ર

ત્ર

End of lesson.

Lesson 9 - U

ઉ, U sounds like a short "oo" as in Hook.

Learn It:

- Think of "oo" in Hook.
- Imagine the sound.
- Pronounce the letter,
- Trace the letter, then write it.

Lesson 9 - U

ઊ	U 2	Moon 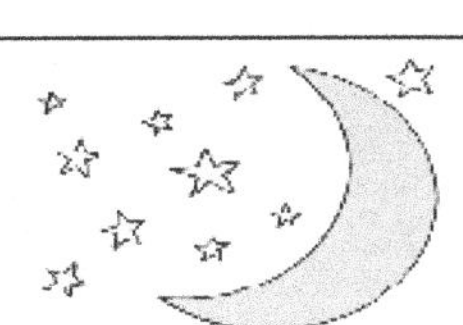

ઊ, U2 is the long "oooo" sound like in "Moon".

Learn It:

- Think of "oo" in Moon.
- Imagine the sound.
- Pronounce the letter,
- Trace the letter, then write it.

ઊ ઊ ઊ ઊ ઊ ઊ ઊ

ઊ ઊ ઊ ઊ ઊ ઊ ઊ

ઊ

ઊ

End of lesson.

Lesson 10 - VWXYZ

વ	V	Vulture

વ, V sounds like the "V" in Vulture.

The letter W words such as Walter and Won, can also be written with the Gujarati વ, V.

Learn It:

- Think of "V" in Vulture.
- Imagine the sound.
- Pronounce the letter.
- Trace the letter, then write it.

વ વ વ વ વ વ વ

વ વ વ વ વ વ વ

વ

વ

Lesson 10 - VWXYZ

ય	Y	Yum

ય, Y sounds like the "Y" in Yum.

Learn It:

- Think of "Y" in Yum.
- Imagine the sound.
- Pronounce the letter,
- Trace the letter, then write it.

ય ય ય ય ય ય ય

ય ય ય ય ય ય ય

ય

ય

Lesson 10 - VWXYZ

ઝ	Z	Czar
ઝ, Z sounds like the "Z" sound in Czar. The letter X words such as Xylophone can also be written with the Gujarati ઝ, Z.	**Learn It:** ○ Think of "z" in Czar. ○ Imagine the sound. ○ Pronounce the letter, ○ Trace the letter, then write it.	

ઝ ઝ ઝ ઝ ઝ ઝ ઝ

ઝ ઝ ઝ ઝ ઝ ઝ ઝ

ઝ

ઝ

End of lesson.

Lesson 11 – A Vowels

આ	A 2	Arm

આ, A2 sounds like a long soft "A" as in Arm, different then the "uh" sound in America. A2 is written like the letter A with a straight line: અ → આ.

Learn It:

- Think of "A" in Arm.
- Imagine the sound.
- Pronounce the letter,
- Trace the letter, then write it.

આ આ આ આ આ આ આ

આ આ આ આ આ આ આ

આ

આ

Lesson 11 - A Vowels

A
3

Aim

એ, A3 sounds like the hard "A" in "Aim". It is written as the A symbol with an accent on top like a backtick above the letter. અ → એ .

Learn It:

- Think of "A" in Aim.
- Imagine the sound.
- Pronounce the letter,
- Trace the letter, then write it.

Lesson 11 - A Vowels

A
4

Aye

ઐ, A4 is a combined "Ai" sound, like a Pirate saying "Aye". This is written as the A symbol with 2 backticks on top. અ → ઐ.

Learn It:

- Think of "Aye".
- Imagine the sound.
- Pronounce the letter,
- Trace the letter, then write it.

Lesson 11 - A Vowels

A
5

Auto

ઔ, A5 is the "Aww" sound as in "Auto". It is written with the addition of an extra line and two backticks. અ → ઔ

Learn It:

- Think of "Au" in Auto.
- Imagine the sound.
- Pronounce the letter,
- Trace the letter, then write it.

ઔ ઔ ઔ ઔ ઔ ઔ ઔ

ઔ ઔ ઔ ઔ ઔ ઔ ઔ

ઔ

ઔ

Lesson 11 - A Vowels

A 6	Umbrella

અં, A6 is a combined "um" sound, as in Umbrella. This is written by taking the A symbol and placing a dot on top of the right-hand line. અ → અં.

Learn It:

- Think of "Um" in Umbrella.
- Imagine the sound.
- Pronounce the letter,
- Trace the letter, then write it.

અં અં અં અં અં અં અં

અં અં અં અં અં અં અં

અં

અં

End of lesson.

Vowel Alternatives

Gujarati has a concept I call vowel alternatives. This is a way of providing the vowel sound to a consonant, without writing the entire vowel letter.

The letter B as you learned above sounds like "buh" as in Bus. What if you wanted to say the word Bee? In Gujarati if you wrote the B and E letters it would sound like "BuhE". Instead, Gujarati allows you to change the ending vowel sound of a consonant. This is done by writing the letter B and adding the vowel alternative for the E sound. We will now review these vowel alternatives in the A, E, I, O, U order.

Lesson 12 - A Vowel Alternatives

બાર	A 2	Bar
A2 sounds like the long "A" in Arm. To say Bar, add the A2 Alternate (a line to the left) to the letter B and get બાર.		**Learn It:** ○ Think of "A" in Arm. ○ Imagine the sound. ○ Pronounce the letter, ○ Trace the letter, then write it.

બાર બાર બાર બાર બાર બાર બાર

બાર બાર બાર બાર બાર બાર બાર

બાર

બાર

Lesson 12 - A Vowel Alternatives

પેય	A 3	Pay

A3 sounds like a hard "A" as in Aim. To say Pay, add the A3 Alternative (a backtick on top) of the letter P and get "પેય ".

Learn It:

- Think of "A" in Aim.
- Imagine the sound.
- Pronounce the letter,
- Trace the letter, then write it.

પેય પેય પેય પેય પેય પેય પેય

પેય પેય પેય પેય પેય પેય પેય

પેય

પેય

Lesson 12 - A Vowel Alternatives

કૈન	A 4	Fine

A4 sounds like "Ai" as in "Aye" by a pirate. To say the word Fine, add the A4 alternative (2 backticks) to the letter F and get "કૈન."

Learn It:

- Think of "ai" in Aye.
- Imagine the sound.
- Pronounce the letter,
- Trace the letter, then write it.

કૈન કૈન કૈન કૈન કૈન કૈન કૈન

કૈન કૈન કૈન કૈન કૈન કૈન કૈન

કૈન

કૈન

Lesson 12 - A Vowel Alternatives

A
5

Four

A5 sounds like "au" as in Auto. To say Four, add the A5 alternative (a line and 2 backticks) and add to the letter F and get "ફૌર."

Learn It:

- Think of "au" in Auto.
- Imagine the sound.
- Pronounce the letter,
- Trace the letter, then write it.

ફૌર ફૌર ફૌર ફૌર ફૌર ફૌર ફૌર

ફૌર ફૌર ફૌર ફૌર ફૌર ફૌર ફૌર

ફૌર

ફૌર

Lesson 12 - A Vowel Alternatives

મં	A 6	Mum

A6 sounds like the "um" in Umbrella. To say Mum, add the A6 alternative (adding a dot on top) to the letter M to get "મં."

Learn It:

- Think of "um" in Umbrella.
- Imagine the sound.
- Pronounce the letter,
- Trace the letter, then write it.

મં મં મં મં મં મં મ

મં મં મં મં મં મં મં

મં

મં

End of lesson.

Lesson 13 - EIOU Vowels

Review the EIOU vowels above, then proceed to Lesson 14.

Lesson 14 - EIOU Vowel Alternatives

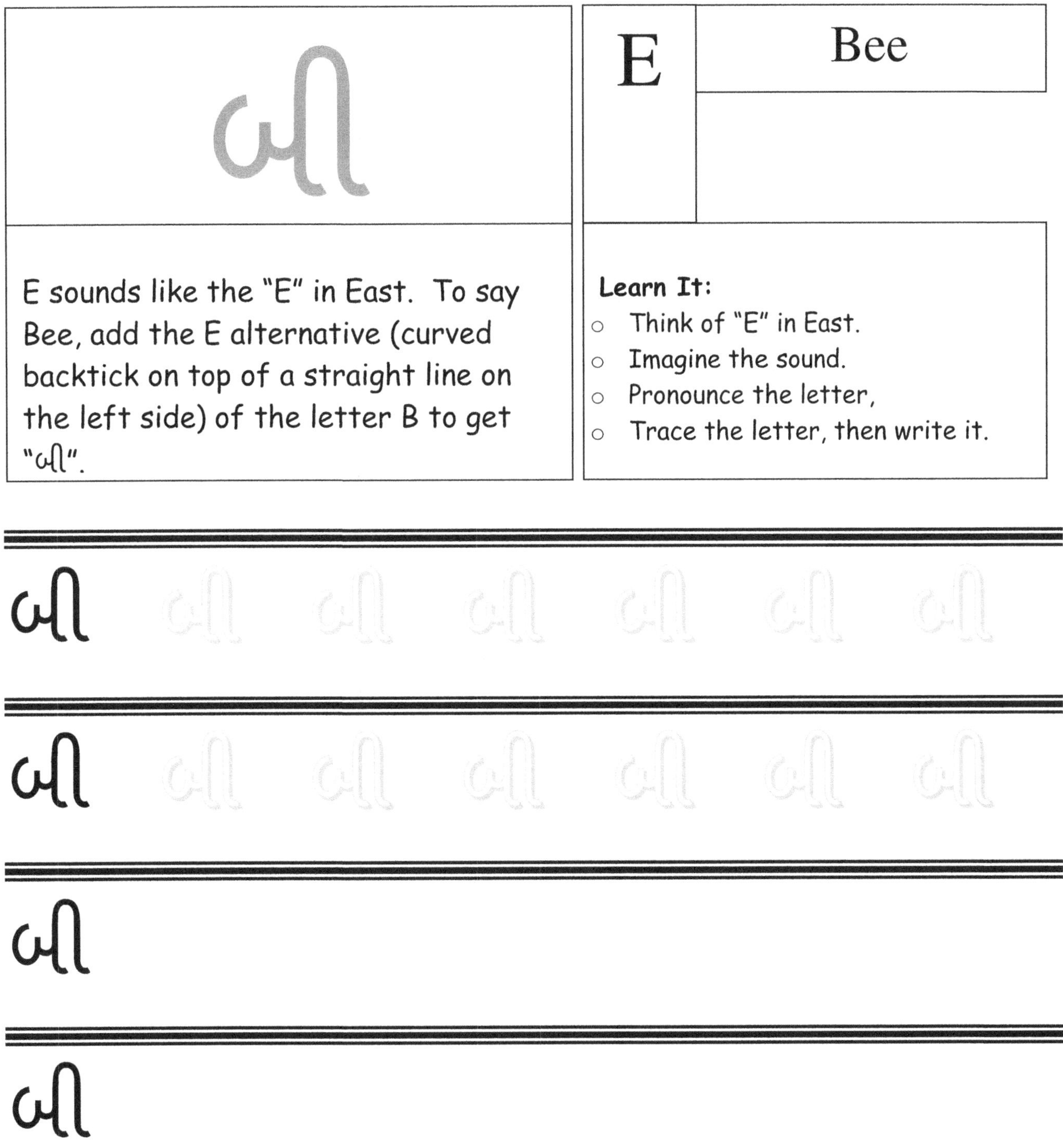

બી

E

Bee

E sounds like the "E" in East. To say Bee, add the E alternative (curved backtick on top of a straight line on the left side) of the letter B to get "બી".

Learn It:

- Think of "E" in East.
- Imagine the sound.
- Pronounce the letter,
- Trace the letter, then write it.

Lesson 14 - EIOU Vowel Alternatives

રિક	I	Rick

I sounds like the "I" in Igloo. To say Rick, add the I alternative (curved backtick on top of a straight line on the right side) of the letter R to get "રિક."

Learn It:

- Think of "I" in Igloo.
- Imagine the sound.
- Pronounce the letter,
- Trace the letter, then write it.

રિક રિક રિક રિક રિક રિક રિક

રિક રિક રિક રિક રિક રિક રિક

રિક

રિક

Lesson 14 - EIOU Vowel Alternatives

O	Road

O sounds like the "O" on Okra. To say Road, add the O alternative (a line and diagonal backtick on the left side) to the letter R to get "રોદ".

Learn It:

- Think of "O" in Okra.
- Imagine the sound.
- Pronounce the letter,
- Trace the letter, then write it.

રોદ રોદ રોદ રોદ રોદ રોદ રોદ

રોદ રોદ રોદ રોદ રોદ રોદ રોદ

રોદ

રોદ

Lesson 14 - EIOU Vowel Alternatives

બુક	U	Book

U sounds like the "oo" as in Hook. To say Book, add the U alternative (curly wave subscript going from right to left) to the letter B to get "બુક".

Learn It:

- Think of "oo" in Hook.
- Imagine the sound.
- Pronounce the letter,
- Trace the letter, then write it.

બુક બુક બુક બુક બુક બુક બુક

બુક બુક બુક બુક બુક બુક બુક

બુક

બુક

Lesson 14 - EIOU Vowel Alternatives

મૂન	U 2	Moon

U2 sounds like the long "oo" in Moon. To say Moon, add the U2 alternative (curly wave subscript going from left to right) to the letter M to get "મૂન".

Learn It:
- Think of "oo" in Moon.
- Imagine the sound.
- Pronounce the letter,
- Trace the letter, then write it.

મૂન મૂન મૂન મૂન મૂન મૂન મૂન

મૂન મૂન મૂન મૂન મૂન મૂન મૂન

મૂન

મૂન

End of lesson.

ABCs of Gujarati Chart

English	Gujarati	Sound	Word	Note
A	અ	Uh	America	Simple A
A2	આ	Aah	Arm	Long A
A3	એ	A	Aim	Strong A
A4	ઐ	Ai	Aye	Long, A with an I combination
A5	ઔ	Aww	Auto	Au variation
A6	અં	Um	Umbrella	A with a U combination
B	બ	Buh	Bus	
B2	ભ	Bh	Bharat	No English equivalent
C	ચ	Ch	Chin	English C - sounds like and S (circle) or K (cut)
C2	છ	Chha	Charge	
D	દ	Duh	Duck	
D2	ડ	Da	Dad	
D3	ઢ	Dh	Dharma	
D4	ધ	The	"The"	
E	ઈ	E	East	
F	ફ	Fuh	Fur	
G	ગ	Guh	Gum	
G2	ઘ	Gh	Ghost	
H	હ	Huh	Hut	
I	ઇ	I	Igloo	Short i
J	જ	Juh	Jug	
K	ક	Kuh	Kazoo	

English	Gujarati	Sound	Word	Note
K2	ખ	Kh	Khan	
K3	ક્ષ	Ksh	Kshtriya	No English equivalent
L	લ	Luh	London	
L2	ળ	(a)La		No English equivalent
M	મ	Muh	Mother	
N	ન	Nuh	Nut	
N2	ણ	(a)Na		No English equivalent
O	ઓ	O	Okra	
P	પ	Puh	Puppy	
Q				substitute K
R	ર	Ruh	Run	
S	સ	Suh	Sun	
S2	શ	Sh	Ship	
S3	ષ	Sha	Shark	
T	ત	T	Tim	
T2	ટ	T	Tom	
T3	ઠ	Tha	Thunder	
T4	થ	Th	Think	
T5	ત્ર	tr	Tres	
U	ઉ	oo	Hook	Short “oo”
U2	ઊ	Oooo	Moon	Long “oo”
V	વ	Vuh	Vulture	
W				substitute V
X				substitute K3 or Z
Y	ય	Yuh	Yum	
Z	ઝ	Zuh	Czar	

Vowel Alternative Chart

English	Gujarati	Sound	Alternate Symbol	Word	Word in Gujarati
A	અ	Uh	*None*	Bud	બદ
A2	આ	Aah	Line on left	Bar	બાર
A3	એ	A	Back tick	Bay	બેય
A4	ઐ	Ai	Double Backtick	Bite	બૈટ
A5	ઔ	Au	Double Backtick and line	Ball	બૌલ
A6	અં	Um	Dot	Bump	બંપ
E	ઈ	E	Curved backtick and line on Right	Bee	બી
I	ઇ	I	Curved backtick and line on Left	Bit	બિટ
O	ઓ	O	Diagonal Backtick and line on Right	Boat	બોટ
U	ઉ	oo	Subscript curly wave going Right to Left	Book	બુક
U2	ઊ	Oooo	Subscript curly wave going Left to Right	Boot	બૂટ

Made in the USA
Las Vegas, NV
20 January 2022